MW01278125

SUNRISE

day one, year 2000

naseem javed

LINKBRIDGE PUBLISHING, NEW YORK, TORONTO

LINKBRIDGE PUBLISHING
New York Toronto

SUNRISE
Day One, Year 2000
Javed, Naseem

Library of Congress
Cataloguing-In-Publication Data
C.I.P. 96-94408

ISBN 0-9639702-2-4

Copyright 1996
Photo: Yousuf Karsh
Design: CORPOMUNDI New York
Printed in Canada

SUNRISE

day one, year 2000

Index

Introduction

One of these days, you will
wake up to the realization
that it is day one, the month
is January and the
year is 2000.

You'll be shocked that
without any Big Bang or
hoopla, you have suddenly
crossed over the threshold
of the new millennium

Introduction

Funny, this so-called
high-speed, fast-paced life
has taken you into a new
transition and slowly places
you into a different time
zone without any apparent

Introduction

However, those who are monitoring the change and its pace will notice that there were some distinct eras in the previous, 20th century, which dominated our total behavior.

There have been several major "periods" which modern communication has gone through.

Introduction

For starters, if knowledge is supposed to be the bond of society, then the printed word was the major breakthrough and the first step. Every executive of the 20th century, challenged to survive, knew well that the germination of ideas and words created demand and needs, resulting in commerce

Introduction

After all, without spreading words and thoughts, there can be no formulation of opinion and the massive need to pursue it.

So how did all of this start, anyway?

Print Society

In the early part of the 20th century, we were still a print society. It was an era of fact-finding, research and writing stories, all of them well-composed and clearly written by the literate few for the select few who could either afford to buy them or had the ability to read them.

Print Society

At the dawn of this period,
there was little or no notion
that somewhere in the
future would be an
advanced society which
might use some forms of

Print Society

In this era,
extraordinary effort was
spent in thinking and
creating written expressions
which would convey all the

Print Society

Nostradamus was still buried among the medieval scriptures.

Sunworshippers were still discovering new gods, and

Print Society

In this period,
print was power, and it
affected everyone.
The future was left alone,
and the information flow
was at a near standstill.
Ma and Pa founded the
small business. Tools of
the trade were the latest
technology, and
Paul Bunyan and Davy
Crockett were the heroes,

Print Society

Movies were silent.

People bought things out of pure necessity, while they struggled to survive.

Work was the biggest motivator, and nickels and dimes in any quantity were the money-making schemes.

Print Society

As American business was dominated by men of passion and drive, these entrepreneurs had vision; they had energy; they had innovative and highly

Print Society

By slapping their last names upon their products, these remarkable men saw their sur-names become part of the world's vocabulary: Heinz, Ford, Gillette, Kraft, Singer, Firestone, and dozens more.

Print Society

The personality of names
of products was created
to look fine in print,
preferably in the same
limited numbers of
typeface available:

Print Society

Names were long,
so they were able to clearly
describe what the business,
product or service
were all about.

Print Society

And every product found
it necessary to assure the
customer of its soundness
and workability, as the
public was justifiably
fearful of poor quality

Radio Society

After centuries of print
came radio.
The emergence of this
audacious and sound-driven
society involved
broadcasting from a select
group to everybody.
And, indeed, everybody
tap-danced to their work,
rocked their heads at the
assembly line, and
fox-trotted home.

Radio Society

The radio had made it possible for any message to be heard, as well as to receive this new message. Literacy was not an issue and what came over the air was free.

Radio Society

Will Rogers provided the humor and Orson Welles demonstrated the power on a Halloween eve with his narration of "War of the Worlds."

Radio Society

In commerce, millions
around the world--both
financiers and the family
next door--were seriously
shaken by the
Stock Market Crash.
Security had now become
the big motivator, big
dollars and bonds were the
money schemes.

Nylon was the killer brand.

Radio Society

When it came to other brand names, the advertising of products exploded. Radio and print both fueled each other, and thrived on the phenomenal

Radio Society

In personality,
business and product names
were developed to have an
audio quality, rather than
merely printed in a typed
form, as in the past.

Radio Society

All this,
while an increasing
amount of information
flowed from the few
to the countless millions.

TV Society

Television combined
pictures and action, and
created colorful interaction,
while exploding
everyone's imagination.

TV Society

That strange black box in the living room worked like a giant magnet, attracting everybody to be glued down, only to be excused to go to the washroom during the programming, because commercials were more enjoyable.

TV Society

First you read, heard on the radio, and then actually saw Walter Winchell and Ed Sullivan.

Suddenly, both ideas and hearsay appeared more real than ever, and right before our eyes.

TV Society

Old myths faded while
new ones came into being;
knowledge increased,
and new visions were
formed.

The Future became
friendly and inviting,
as never before.

TV Society

In commerce, both technicolor movies and color TV opened the eyes and the imagination, as seeing Cleopatra in bed

TV Society

The flow of products and
new brands mushroomed in
every aspect of our lives.
Maybe that is why people
discovered running:
Running to
or running from.
This health craze, in turn,
led to new products for
wiser eating habits and
lifestyles.

TV Society

The biggest motivator was
power, and more power.

Business became big,
corporations bigger,
bureaucracy became
the standard,
monopolies the status.
Big was beautiful.
People worked for power
and security and invested
heavily in the markets.

TV Society

In branding, while the
media exploded, Xerox
facilitated reproduction of
copies, Polaroid worked to
capture the moment, while
Sony provided recording
cassettes for our greater
listening pleasure

TV Society

In personality, the
information flow was from
many to many, and brand
names, for the first time,
were designed to convey
the power of color and their
visual impact.

Computer Society

Copper wire and giant tubes
were dead, transistors and
silicon chips were in:
the electronic age had
arrived, bringing logical
interaction at lightning
speed from all directions

Computer Society

In commerce, in contrast
to the earlier struggles of
survival and painful
undertakings to launch the
Industrial Revolution,
this new age was born in

Computer Society

And haphazard, redundant
techno-babble created the
new computer terminology,
as the languages of the
world were filled with
everything from

Computer Society

IBM provided
the battlefield,
Apple the sword.
The Computer War had
begun, and information
was now flowing from

Computer Society

This logically-driven society projected data at ferocious speeds with great accuracy and control, breaking mythical boundaries, proving facts,

Computer Society

The force of information
was awesome, which
created massive
reorganization and made
the disks spin.
Small change was out,

Computer Society

So were the letters Q and R:
Quality of life, Quality of
operations, and Quality of
quality, followed by
Re-Invent, Re-define,
and Re-engineer.
Part-timers worked
flex-time, while aerobics
and video games caused
repetitive strain injury.
Miniaturization blossomed.
Micro became beautiful

Telecom Society

Networking created the
Internet-ers, and universal
access came at last.

Information could now
flow from all to one,

Telecom Society

Electronic transmission of
day-to-day commerce was
now moving the white,
blue, and pink collars aside
and putting steel collars on
the robots, along with
desktop junkies, while
corporations miniaturized

Telecom Society

In commerce, flattened
hierarchy, clearly visible in
now-empty skyscrapers,
filled the North American
landscape and dominated the
power shift.

Robocop was almost a
reality, with Bill Gates as
the new icon of fame
and power.

Telecom Society

In this frantic era of hi-tech breakthroughs and media explosions on all fronts, print, radio, TV, computer and the Internet magically took us everywhere, from a

Telecom Society

In branding, as never before in the history of civilization, confusion in communication in the marketplace was glaringly evident.

Telecom Society

Desk-hopping and debit
cards were in, as one hour
of commercial transmission
in the city of New York
represented the entire
economic dialogue of the
19th century.

Telecom Society

At the same time, very large groups of digitally privileged, if somewhat intellectually-challenged, men and women were being formed, and all of a sudden a fear of being everywhere and nowhere at the same time became an issue.

Telecom Society

One minute you could
be in a totally-isolated
mountain retreat;
in the next, you could
be on a videoconference

Telecom Society

In personality, brand names
were developed to not only
convey typography, but also
how they sounded and
projected in color and on
computer screens and at

Virtual Society

If knowledge is the bond
of society, and the printed
word was the breakthrough,
flow and control of
information now have more

Virtual Society

In order to appreciate the
pace of change and the rate
of its growth,
imagine if Alexander the
Great had a cellular phone.

Or if Moses had
desk-top publishing.

Virtual Society

Life will revolve around
multi-media images which
will absorb the total mind
and the total body with
every sensory perception,
and then flood them with

Virtual Society

This purportedly immobile, stationary society will spend time in a visual interaction with everything that each individual mind desires, with their bodies strapped into strange modular contraptions like an astronaut.

Virtual Society

Brands will be more global
than ever, as will be the
businesses and the workers,
with people working
electronically in several
countries around the globe
in the same afternoon.
The number of powerful
global mega-brands will
increase, along with the
number of flags and the
number of new nations.

Virtual Society

Flourishing democracies
will have unique global
branding and identities.

The imagination will have
power, visual image will

Virtual Society

Virtual society may seem enthralling, but it may not move fast enough!

Recall how the wheel came out of the caves?

Virtual Society

Now this micro-cyber revolution looks over a barren landscape of technology, much as the wheel must have done, before getting itself molded into millions of applications all over the world, and going full circle.

Virtual Society

Welcome to the cyber-farm!
Meet the info-baron,
a casual thinker but also
a big Team Player in
a floating corporation,
drifting invisibly
somewhere in cyber-space!
Thinking -- a luxury which
demands time, peace and
isolation -- may actually
return to modern society
after years of absence

Virtual Society

It is now the calm

Virtual Society

And they are working --
and living -- on-line, in the
face-to-face interaction with
large flat screens, enjoying
virtual entertainment
and travel, in an almost
symbionic interphase
of human with
electro-ergonomics.

Virtual Society

The status quo
of bureaucracy will be
seriously challenged,
leading to a kind
of hierarchical meltdown,
with business, government,
major institutions,
and even the media
blurring out of focus.

Virtual Society

Those who are organized
and prepared, will enjoy
the new powers and
a dramatically improved
quality of life.

Virtual Society

How to sum up an
era of such global,
speed-of-light change?

Virtual Society

Shock yourself
at your own risk:
imagine a work model
where there are no
office towers, no bosses.

Virtual Society

Downtown quiets
as work assignments
are delivered
to the workers in their
preferred habitat.

Virtual Society

The wonderful cities and
work models of today are
off-target, and while they
may appear like shining
jewels as seen from the
space shuttle, down on
earth, they are disappearing
like the long-vanished
Seven Wonders
of the World.

Conclusion

In the very near future,
things will not be cut and
dry, black and white,
big or small.

Conclusion

Maybe, like
factorial geometry,
we may create a factorial
society, wherein everything
will shape itself
into its own true form:
like three-dimensional
rainbows, an exploding
universe in color, where
people may well start
searching for new gods
all over again.

Conclusion

In branding,
this new society could
well gobble up single
global icons like a giant
bowl of cereal, every single
minute, and a small number
of elite global brands will
dominate the entire world.

Conclusion

Governments, institutions,
businesses--even a single
individual--will not be able
to hide anything.
The accessibility and the
accountability of every
single action will be in
everybody's view.

This will necessarily
bring reforms.

Conclusion

In commerce, businesses
will survive only as global
players. Microsoft could
appear like a small
pioneering giant of this
period. Media moguls will
control the multi-facetted,
multi-dimensional services
provided to sophisticated
customers on a
multi-national basis

Conclusion

Living in color

Conclusion

So what should you do?

Conclusion

Quo Vadis?
Whither goest thou?
Come the year 2000, you may
be on top of a skyscraper in
a penthouse office, or on a
safari trail. Drifting in a hi-tech
boathouse, or counting
pigeons in Central Park.
Tap-dancing on a boardroom
table, or exchanging glances
with a gorilla in the Zoo.
Be prepared!

Conclusion

Meanwhile,
forget Big Management;
simply manage yourself.

After all, by now,
shouldn't we be slightly more
evolved homo sapiens?

Re-discover your hobbies and
improve them to perfection.
Hobbies are talents--
and they are free.

Conclusion

Ignore the noise.
That repetitive, confusing
loud rhetoric coming from
all directions.
Discover silence.
Learn to swim

Conclusion

Remember the
Hard Assets mentality?
Truckload of fertilizer.
Ton of cubic zirconia.
Shipload of mainframes.
Fields of tulips.

Conclusion

Select a thinking and working style, whether in hard, soft or invisible assets.

Conclusion

Such as developing
corporate protocols for
world-wide-cyber-work-force
for the super info-highway.
Or designing systems for
instantaneous color output of
imagination in a digitized form.
How about writing a program
with a billion lines of code on
a CD, designed to replace the
entire bureaucracy of
a G7 country.

Conclusion

Look around and see.
Ideally you must be
a multi-skilled, multi-
talented, multi-national type
of personality with complex
interests, eccentric hobbies,

Conclusion

Consider opening up
an old-fashioned book.
Just don't forget your blue suit.
After all, this earth is large
enough to allow us all
to co-exist in our different
time zones and the different
societies of our century.
So get on with your life,
and enjoy the sunrise.

Charts & Notes

The following charts are for each passing period, from the early printed word to the up-coming cyber-life.

WHAT WAS I DOING?

_____

_____

_____

_____

_____

PRINT SOCIETY

INFO-FLOW:	*From few to several*
BUSINESS:	*Ma & Pa & Small*
MOTIVATORS:	*Muscle & Work*
MONEY SCHEMES:	*Victory Bonds*
FAME & POWER:	*Paul Bunyan, Davy Crockett*
MOVIES:	*Silent, Charlie Chaplin*
MAGAZINES:	*Look, National Geographic*
FASHION:	*Pleats, Suspenders*
PAST-TIMES:	*Chess, Mechano*
AUTOS:	*Model Ts & Fishers*
EATING HABITS:	*Foods & Fats*
BUYING HABITS:	*Basic Goods*
NEW BRANDS:	*Gillette, Arm & Hammer*

WHAT WAS I DOING?

_____

_____

_____

_____

_____

RADIO SOCIETY

IINFO-FLOW:	*From few to many*
BUSINESS:	*Small & Big*
MOTIVATORS:	*Work & Security*
MONEY SCHEMES:	*Bonds & Stocks*
FAME & POWER:	*Tarzan, Nat King Cole*
MOVIES:	*Citizen Kane, Gone With the Wind*
MAGAZINES:	*Time, Life, Playboy*
FASHION:	*Wide Lapel, Blue*
PAST-TIMES:	*Monopoly, Eating*
AUTOS:	*Cadillacs & Rolls*
EATING HABITS:	*Proteins & Fats*
BUYING HABITS:	*Life Necessities*
NEW BRANDS:	*Nylon, IBM*

NOTES:

WHAT WAS I DOING?

_____

_____

_____

_____

_____

TV SOCIETY

INFO-FLOW:	*From many to many*
BUSINESS:	*Big & Corporate*
MOTIVATORS:	*Power & Security*
MONEY SCHEMES:	*Stocks & Bonds*
FAME & POWER:	*Howard Hughes, Elvis*
MOVIES:	*Cleopatra, Ben-Hur*
MAGAZINES:	*Esquire, Rolling Stone*
FASHION:	*Mini, Maxi, Psychedelic*
PAST-TIMES:	*Trivial Pursuit, Running*
AUTOS:	*Mercedes & V8s*
EATING HABITS:	*Proteins & Vegetables*
BUYING HABITS:	*Brands & Luxury Items*
NEW BRANDS:	*Xerox, Polaroid*

NOTES:

WHAT WAS I DOING?

_____

_____

_____

_____

_____

COMPUTER SOCIETY

INFO-FLOW:	*From many to all*
BUSINESS:	*Small & Corporate*
MOTIVATORS:	*Part Time & Flex Time*
MONEY SCHEMES:	*Junk Bonds*
FAME & POWER:	*Steve Jobs, Trump*
MOVIES:	*Jaws, Star Wars*
MAGAZINES:	*People, Inc.*
FASHION:	*Black, Body Suit*
PAST-TIMES:	*Video Games, Aerobics*
AUTOS:	*Mini-Vans & Compacts*
EATING HABITS:	*Nuts & Fiber*
BUYING HABITS:	*Brands, Symbols & Status*
NEW BRANDS:	*Apple, Microsoft*

WHAT WAS I DOING?

_____

_____

_____

_____

_____

TELECOM SOCIETY

INFO-FLOW:	*From all to one & From one to all*
BUSINESS:	*Micro-Corporate & Giant Non-Hierarchical*
MOTIVATORS:	*No-where-ness & Every-where-ness*
MONEY SCHEMES:	*Mutual Funds*
FAME & POWER:	*Bill Gates, Mortal Kombat*
MOVIES:	*Robocop, E.T.-Interactive*
MAGAZINES:	*Wired, VR*
FASHION:	*Grunge, Casual*
PAST-TIMES:	*CyberSurfing, Outdoors*
AUTOS:	*4WDs & V8s*
EATING HABITS:	*Fiber & Cola*
BUYING HABITS:	*Global Brands & Status*
NEW BRANDS:	*Nintendo, CNN*

NOTES:

WHAT *SHOULD* I BE DOING?

_____

_____

_____

_____

_____

VIRTUAL SOCIETY

INFO-FLOW:	*Flooding & Mass Drowning*
BUSINESS:	*Invisible, Micro-Giant Corporations*
MOTIVATORS:	*Privacy & Secrecy Motivated*
MONEY SCHEMES:	*High Risk Info-Ventures*
FAME & POWER:	*You or Me*
MOVIES:	*Custom Movies*
MAGAZINES:	*On-line Delivery*
FASHION:	*Novo-Formal & Formal*
PAST-TIMES:	*Thinking & Eye Rubbing*
AUTOS:	*Hummers & Tri-Wheelers*
EATING HABITS:	*International Menu*
BUYING HABITS:	*Mega-Universal Brands*
NEW BRANDS:	*Netscape, Pixar*

Author

Nearly two decades ago, Naseem Javed founded ABC Namebank International, a corporate name development company in New York and Toronto. He advises CEOs of Fortune 500 and other leading corporations on the strategic roles of corporate and brand names on the global scene. He lectures frequently on issues of business naming. He has also written "Naming for Power: Creating Successful Names for the Business World."

Naseem Javed
javed@ftn.net
www.naseemjaved.com
www.abcnamebank.com